HOW TO DEAL WITH A CHEATING HUSBAND

HANDLING INFIDELITY AND LACK OF TRUST IN MARRIAGE WITHOUT LOSING YOUR MIND

By

Claire Robin

1

Copyright

Dedication

This book is dedicated to all the people in committed relationships and marriage. We all need each other to be strong, and trust is the strongest anchor that holds two people together. Everything revolves around our deepest desires to be happy, and to find someone special to share the same dreams. I hope you will find the good words, guide and the strength you need as you consume this book. Thank you.

Table of Contents

INTRODUCTION

Having to deal with a cheating partner can never be a beautiful experience and it is not one to be wished on anyone. However, life is filled with ups and downs, beautiful experiences and ugly ones alike, one of which is being faced with the pain of betrayal and broken trust in your marriage.

You may just want to end it because of hurt, lies and your inability to see a way forward in your union. This is normal as people deal with pain differently, but taking a step backward to reflect on a lot of things would be the ideal action to take in a case of infidelity.

The society especially in America makes cheating on the side of men seem normal, and cheating on the side of women a taboo. Therefore, when a woman cries out about infidelity by her husband, everyone wants to talk her down or ask her to fight for her home quietly. But they ignore the emotional trauma the wife must be facing as a result of her husband's unfaithfulness. It is surely not going to be easy to remain calm, or to handle such a situation with as much stability as you can muster, but it is possible. However, you don't have to swallow in your pain or neglect your wellbeing in the process of fighting to save your marriage. In this book, we hope to provide you with ways in which you can cope with a cheating husband.

CHAPTER 1: THE EMOTIONS SURROUNDING MARRIAGE INFIDELITY

THE EMOTIONS SURROUNDING MARRIAGE INFIDELITY

Extra marital affairs when discovered can severely ruin marital relationships. This does not mean that infidelity has no effect on the home while the cheating partner is yet to be found out. One of the issues with cheating is you live with the fear of being caught, and will likely have to keep covering up your tracks with lies.

When a man is involved in extra marital affairs, the tendency of neglecting his family is high as he is torn between being present for his wife, kids, and his cheating partner. Though in most cases men who cheat end up being remorseful, in rare cases some of these men do not feel remorseful when caught neither are they scared of being found out by their wives.

This is usually the case in a marriage where the husband has little or no regard for the feelings of his wife. Some of the emotions that can be spurred in a home where either of the partner is found cheating are anger, hurt, sense of betrayal, mistrust, guilt, and hatred or repulsion.

It is very difficult to manage these emotions as they are only natural feelings resulting from the betrayal of a loved one you must have trusted deeply. In some cases, women who already believe their husbands capable of cheating tend to swallow the hurt better than women who had believed with all their hearts that their spouse was incapable of breaking their trust. Having years of promises and vows hit this rough spot can be extremely devastating for the hurt partner and will shake the roots of the union immensely.

Anger is a vast emotion, and very powerful too. It pushes us to take actions we may end up regretting for life. One of the first things a wife going through this hurt needs to be told, is to not take any actions based on her emotions. It is very true that the heart has a mind of its own, and being betrayed would spark up a million emotions especially when you have to see the person who betrayed you every single day. But resolving to actions that will cause more hurt in your home and possibly affect the lives of your children, should be an absolute no.

The tension between couples can easily be sensed by the kids especially in a home where both parents are very fond of each other. So before you go all wild as a wife on your cheating husband, think about your children.

Another person to consider, is yourself. Your health is of utmost importance to you and those around you. Anger tends to cause more harm to the person nursing it, than the person guilty of the crime. So make it a priority to maintain or regain calmness, and take decisions when you are in a healthy state of mind.

Researches show that many men tend to resort to violence when they catch their wives being unfaithful, especially if she is caught in the act with her cheating partner. There are also cases of men who choose to walk out of their wives or send her packing as their own reaction to her unfaithfulness.

Women on the other hand can also react violently especially at their husband's mistress, but afterwards break down emotionally. This does not mean that men do not break down too, but the woman has a higher tendency of an emotional outburst than the man. Men often resort to seething and silent fury, while women choose a much more expressive way to show their hurt.

CHAPTER 2: WHAT TO DO IF YOU SUSPECT YOUR HUSBAND IS CHEATING

WHAT TO DO IF YOU SUSPECT YOUR HUSBAND IS CHEATING

Nobody enjoys being lied to, and men as well as women would feel deeply betrayed if they discovered that their partner broke their trust. The feeling of hurt in this case is not gender specific. However, this book is centered on helping wives cope with cheating husbands.

When trust starts being questioned in a marriage, it becomes an indication that the marriage is headed down a rough path as love without trust cannot work. A mere suspicion of your husband's unfaithfulness is never enough grounds to confront him with as this may adversely affect your marriage if your hunch turns out wrong. Inasmuch as no one enjoys being lied to, no one enjoys being doubted by those they truly love especially when they are staying true to their promises. Giving your husband the impression that you do not trust him will hurt and eventually affect your union.

Suspicion in the first place indicates a lack of trust from you as the wife unless in a situation where you have been given good reasons to question your husband's faithfulness to you. In this case, there are few steps you can take to either prove your suspicion right or wrong. It would be best to not jump into conclusions or accusations till you've taken these steps and come to a sure conclusion that your husband is either cheating, or not.

i)   Calm down:

You might be wondering how this helps but experiences and time have proven that humans do not exactly make rational decisions when they're highly emotional. The first thing you want to do when you have your suspicions, is to calm down and reflect on things. It is in the best interest of your marriage that you rethink your actions before you take them. Taking time to relax and reflect might even make you realize you made a big deal out of nothing in the first place. But this doesn't mean you should doubt your instincts or the signs you noticed if they still prove strong after you have thought them through.

The need to be in a stable state of mind and not act just based on your emotions, is emphasized here again. After you're sure you're stable, move on to the next step.

ii)   Examine further:

This step is necessary, because you do not want to confront your partner with no evidence. Go back to whatever it is you saw that made you suspicious and investigate it further. This also helps to put off confronting him at all in a case where he is actually being faithful to you.

Looking deeper into whatever might have sparked up suspicion does not mean a license to stalk your partner or snoop around his messages. Your husband is not dumb and will eventually find out if you cross the line into stalking him.

This will lead to a confrontation when you're not at all prepared for it. In the most discreet way, investigate further into the call or message you might have come across to make you suspicious of your partner, without giving him a reason to question you.

However this turns out, you have to be sure you are ready to find out the truth because it might be worse than you thought, or thankfully, you might have been wrong about everything. Know when to accept the truth and stop probing so you don't ruin a beautiful marriage with suspicions.

iii) Talk:

Communication has proven to be one of the most effective tool in relationships. The power of sincere conversations cannot be over emphasized. If your investigation proves your suspicion true, or gave you reasons to believe the possibility of infidelity in your marriage, the next wise thing to do is to confront your partner.

How you handle this will go a long way. You do not have to accuse your husband flatly, you can bring to his notice the concerns you are having and the evidence that fueled them. A man who loves you in this case would have reasons for a rethink if actually he is cheating or considering doing so.

You have to make the conversation completely honest and also keep an open heart. Most women start conversations with accusations and this keeps your husband in a defensive state throughout the conversation, and ruins the purpose of this step. Don't go in all blinded by anger, go calm.

If you handle this wisely, your husband would open up to you if he loves you, rather than go into a fight with you. Words are delicate tools, they can either open a heart or shut them. In a case where you value your marriage and want to fix it no matter what the truth turns out to be, you want a partner that is remorseful and equally ready to work to fix whatever has been broken in your union.

At this point, you should know when your husband is lying to you from his reactions and your instincts. Many men have mastered the act of lying though, but you would want to watch him closely and be sure he is being completely honest.

Another thing to watch is your reaction. Give him time to open up to you without shutting him down or discouraging him from doing so with your outbursts.

This talk is not necessarily meant for when your husband turns out to actually be cheating. You can also have this conversation to address your concerns about certain actions or people who made you feel suspicious of him. Good communication works like miracle and is very essential in a happy home whether there's a case of suspicion or not.

Make daily and intimate conversations a habit, and watch your home bloom.

iv)   Revisit boundaries:

If your talk with your partner proves him innocent, then there is still a need nonetheless for you both to discuss your boundaries with third parties. Whatever it is that may have raised doubts in your heart should be addressed.

Be it colleagues at work, employees, friends or acquaintances that may have come into the picture, state the things that made you uncomfortable, and discuss readjustment with your partner. You should also be ready to hear from him because there might be adjustments needed to be made on your part too. You would both have to set or revisit the lines that should not be crossed with outsiders or third parties to prevent crisis and suspicion in your union.

If on the other hand your partner is cheating, you might turn out to be devastated and may not be in the right frame of mind to take any decisions at that point. But do not forget that your partner opened up to you, and this may be a sign he is willing to turn away from his illicit affairs.

You would still need space to get yourself together, time to heal, and lots of reflecting to do. In this case, decide if you would want to handle things on your own or involve a counsellor to help you both work through your healing process.

A marriage is always worth fighting for, especially if the defaulter is sincerely sorry. Do not be too fast to give up on your union, but do not be too fast to say you've forgiven too. Give yourself time, and heal gradually. People either make the mistake of leaving too quickly or saying they've forgiven too fast. In both cases, regrets might arise again in time to come. So take it easy on making any decision, and remember to first take things easy on yourself.

CHAPTER 3: HOW TO BE SURE IF YOUR HUSBAND IS ACTUALLY CHEATING

HOW TO BE SURE IF YOUR HUSBAND IS ACTUALLY CHEATING

It wouldn't come as a surprise if some women try the first three steps stated above only to meet a dead end with no answers at all. Some men are very tricky and smart, and might just put up a show when you confront them instead of being truly honest with you. Some may even go as far as making you feel guilty for confronting them when actually, they're cheating on you.

This is usually the case with men who are intentionally bent on cheating on their wives, or who may have intentions of abandoning her for their mistress. If all forms of honesty do not push your husband to change or say the truth, then you have to be very careful and mindful of your own safety.

However, if you've tried the steps above only to end up more confused, then these few signs might be indications that your husband is truly cheating on you.

i) Secrecy:

When you notice that your husband has become secretive with calls, texts and outings, this might mean he has something he's hiding from you. It might be another woman, or a shady deal he has gotten himself involved in. Watch out for this sign in your husband especially if he was someone that had no issue with you taking his calls only to suddenly become uneasy with leaving his phone just lying around in the house. Also, your partner should have no issue with telling you where he is at given times especially if your communication level is good. When he starts having issues with telling you of his whereabouts, it's a red flag.

ii) Lack of emotional attachment:

Naturally, men love to be shown attention by their wives. It is said that women have major roles to play in the lives of men at every stage of their lives and as his wife, this duty falls ultimately on you. If your husband no longer craves your attention or a bond with you, if he's totally fine with halfhearted conversations and little or no together time, chances are he is forming all of these attachments with someone else. Women in some cases also play a role in the negative here. They do not realize the essence of their attention and care in the lives of their husbands and sometimes are emotionally unavailable to him. Being emotionally unavailable to your husband poses a big risk and makes him vulnerable to the ladies lurking around. This doesn't mean you should retire into self-blame or let anyone make you feel guilty for the ill doings of your husband. There is no justification for cheating, and this would be a very bad time to start blaming yourself.

iii) Unnecessary irritation or anger:

One of the famous lines cheating husbands tell their mistresses is that they do not know why they married their wives in the first place.

Once a married man starts getting involved with another woman especially intentionally with no remorse, then he most likely spends his time trying to convince her that he loves and values her more than his wife. Your husband might start to show irritation at your slightest mistakes and angry outbursts in some cases. This might lead you to start doubting yourself, finding faults in yourself, and questioning what it is you're doing wrong. Understand that it is not always because you're doing something wrong that a man cheats on you. It is his own shortcoming and decision to break the vows he made to you especially if he is not sorry for his actions. An unnecessary increased irritation by your husband towards you, might just be a sign that he's having an illicit affair with another woman, and thereby sees you as the enemy in his way. Some men also resolve to this when they're torn between their wife and their mistress. The anger and frustration can just be a result of their confusion and lack of ideas on how to come out from the extra marital affair they have involved themselves in.

iv) Absence:

When your husband forms a habit of being continuously absent in the home, this might just indicate that someone else has got his attention. He begins to keep late nights, spends more time at work or in the office, has extended meetings, goes on increased business trips and is not bothered about the effect it has on his wife or kids. If you try talking to him about it and he cuts down his absence for a while only to go back to it again, this is a glaring pointer that your husband might be having an affair. Having a sexual relationship with a woman outside the bonds of marriage, can become an addiction and even when the men involved would want to turn away from it, it can prove very difficult. Which is why some men are unable to end their illicit relationships till they are caught. It is not easy to be fully available for one woman, so when they become two or more, the slack in being present for your wife becomes very obvious.

v) Lack of sexual intimacy:

We pointed to emotional attachment first before highlighting the place of sex because even though sex might be the strongest form of intimacy, it is not the only form of intimacy. There are also men who have no issues being sexually active with their wives even while they cheat on her. So if your husband falls in this category, it is left for you to look out for other signs. This does not mean that majority of men do not suddenly become less sexually active with their wives once they start cheating. Your husband should not just stop showing interest in you or desiring you. If he does, then something is certainly wrong and should be sought out. Do not neglect it or turn a blind eye to this sign, if you notice it in your home. Wives are advised to talk to their husbands first about this, before jumping into conclusions if it's the only sign you notice. Men may tend to not crave sex as much due to other reasons such as stress at work, a major setback he might be keeping to himself, medical issues and the likes. So make it a point to find out the reason behind your husband's withdrawal.

vi) Increased amount of gifts:

This might sound funny but it is also a sign your husband might be cheating on you and is trying to push off the feeling of guilt by showing you with gifts.

It is important to always not jump into conclusions as most men eventually cultivate this habit just to show sincere love for their wives. But if your husband gets you this gifts only when he has fails to meet up with appointments or dates you two set together, when he goes on numerous trips and fails to be present for you and the kids, when he is continuously absent and emotionally distant, then they might just be his way of making himself feel better for the wrong he is doing, or making you distracted from his shortcomings.

CHAPTER 4: STEPS TO DEALING WITH ANGER AND DISAPPOINTED EMOTIONS

STEPS TO DEALING WITH ANGER AND DISAPPOINTED EMOTIONS

Once you've confirmed that your husband is cheating on you, or maybe find out without prior suspicions, the feeling of anger and disappointment would set in. Hurt and pain would likely overwhelm you and leave you in a state of confusion. It won't be easy deciding if you want to stay and fight to build back the walls of your home or if you want to leave. Naturally, you would consider packing up and leaving your cheating husband alone. But a more rational thought might make you decide to stay back and at least try. Deciding to stay back, would mean you did not let the anger get the best of you. This does not mean that if you reacted too angrily it is too late to try and work things out, no it is not. As long as your husband is also willing to fix your marriage, it is worth giving a try.

Here are few steps that can help you calm down after discovering you've been betrayed by your partner:

i) Take time away to calm down:

Being around your husband at this period may not really be the best thing to do. You would need time to yourself, time to reflect on a lot of things and decide if you want to still fight for your home and why. Time away from him also gives you the space to deal with the hurt without having to be reminded by his presence every day. It is normal to feel really angry and equally normal to want to lash out, and seeing him continuously while the hurt is still deep would only feed this feeling. How long you stay away from him too is another thing to not stretch too long. You want time to calm down, but you cannot run away from the reality of your home for too long. Go back home especially if you want to make your marriage work again and put in your best to fix it. In some cases, it is the man who offers to leave till the wife is healed enough to have him back at home. Whichever you both decide to do, do not let it stretch for too long.

ii) Talk to someone:

Talking is a good therapy and at this point, you would really need someone to vent your feelings. Someone you can trust to not cause more damage to your home with the news. Family members are not the best option in this case as they may not forgive your husband for his mistakes even after you do, and friends unless one you completely trust, may not be the best option either. A therapist is advised because your discussions stays confidential and they handle the issue professionally. However, you might want to share your problems with someone you have an emotional bond with, not a counsellor, and this is good for you too. Talk to a friend you completely trust, and ask that it stays between you two. If you prefer family, then pick someone you can share things with without it spreading to the entire family. Do not try to be all strong and self-sufficient at this point else you might break down. For the sake of your wellbeing and that of your home, find someone you can confide in, and do so. Pour out your feelings, cry if you need to, then move on to work things out with your partner as you would feel better after this.

iii) Accept the truth and face it head on:

It is not going to be easy to accept that someone you could have literally risked your life for betrayed you. Acceptance here does not come in your crying and wondering where you ever went wrong, it is in embracing the fact that it has happened, and that cannot be changed. However, the fact that it happened does not mean that it should keep happening or cannot be fixed. Look for means to move on from the point of the betrayal, as drowning in it will not help you or your home. There are actions to take to put things back in place and you cannot do any of these if you're still nursing your pain or mourning the broken trust between your partner and yourself.

iv) Do things to make yourself happy:

It is true that when we feel let down, we instinctively want to just lock ourselves up in our rooms, separate ourselves from the world and cry our souls out. It's okay to be emotional, it's part of being human. But after taking your time to cry and go through countless rounds if self-pity, it's time to step out and do beautiful things for yourself too. You can involve in activities and hobbies that you're passionate about. You can hang out with your group of friends, go on picnics, tours, or evening sit outs. A temporary distraction to heal yourself before facing the responsibility ahead of you is beautiful too. This also reminds you that it's not the end of the world, and that there are other beautiful sides to life than a painful betrayal. Remember that there is nothing wrong with you, and you deserve every good thing that life has to offer.

CHAPTER 5: STEPS TO DEALING WITH AN UNFAITHFUL HUSBAND

STEPS TO DEALING WITH AN UNFAITHFUL HUSBAND

Being cheated on is heartbreaking and it is never easy to find complete healing from this break of trust. It would take time, commitment to fixing things, and patience. Do not expect anything to happen overnight, and do not jump into settlements.

Sometimes we tend to undermine the weight of an experience on our emotional wellbeing, and the effect it has on us. We should learn to treat our hearts with as much care as we give the rest of our body or even more. Pushing yourself to do things you're not yet comfortable with just because you want to skip processes and get over the hurt of betrayal as quickly as possible will do more harm than good. Take the steps necessary for your healing, because it is important to you. At the end, you will be thankful you didn't rush into either leaving your marriage or forgiving the hurt too quickly.

Remember that your husband's willingness to work on your marriage together with you will go a long way and make things easier. However, if he is unrepentant and unwilling to fix all that his action has broken, then it's left for you to fight for your own wellbeing.

If you've calmed down to reflect on things and have decided that your marriage is worth saving, then here are few steps that will help you cope with the process.

i)   Start with clarity:

Before you take any steps further, you want to clarify things with your partner. You want to hear from him and be sure he is willing to turn a new leaf, as well as fight for your union with you. Do not go ahead assuming his opinions on the matter, hear from him and be sure the communication with his cheating partner has completely been cut off. This gives you the room to ask questions on things you need to know too. But be careful not to pry too much so you don't end up hurting yourself more with the information you get. Remember that your problem or concern is not the other woman, so do not start putting your energy into finding out details about her. Instead focus on your husband and make things better. Women tend to focus on finding out about the other woman, stalking and even comparing themselves with her. This would only hurt you and make you believe there were certain qualities you lacked that your husband found in her. This is also a threat to your self-esteem and confidence as a woman. It is not your fault that your husband cheated, it is not a result of any shortcomings you have or had, it is a decision he made on his own as there is no justification for marriage infidelity. If you have questions you deeply need answers to, ask your husband. Just don't poke too deep into information that would only hurt you instead of helping at this point. It is essential that you and your spouse maintain having these heartfelt conversations during the whole healing process and even after that. This is a good time to talk, talk about everything. How to fix your home, how to make it better, how to rebuild your bond, things that are not allowed in your marriage when a third party is involved.

ii)   Get tested:

Whether or not you and your partner are standing on the same ground, the next wise thing to do is to immediately get tested for STDs and start treatments if necessary. This might be embarrassing to you, but it is essential. You and your partner alike will have to go through this process together, especially if you have agreed to work things out.

In a case where he refused to, then go ahead and get tested as you do not want your wellbeing to be neglected just because of another person. If your husband refuses to get tested or undergo treatments where necessary, this simply means your wellbeing is of no importance to him and he poses a risk to you if you both become sexually involved again. Make it clear to him that for things to work out between you two, he has to willingly go through the processes of healing with you. The truth is healing would be much easier on you if your husband is willing to become a team with you again, and work on your union. Keep an open heart and mind as you undergo this process, do not resolve to healing blames on him if the results come out positive. Instead focus on getting your treatments and getting better. Some sexually transmitted diseases would be easier to cure than the others, and it would not be easy to forgive him especially with the increased number of troubles you have to go through because of his mistake. But remind yourself constantly why you're doing this in the first place, and keep in sight what is more important to you.

iii)   Visit a Therapist:

After going through the first process, you and your partner will need help taking things back to normal. It is not everyone that has the ability to recover from such a hurt solely on their own, and it is not always advised too. There are families whose Pastor stand as their counsellor, and that's fine too. Just ensure that if you've noticed the need for a matured and professional hand to step in, you allow just that. A therapist means a therapist and not just random people. Remember that you're going through this stage because you want to save your marriage and letting people in on your husband's mistake will pose not only a present risk, but a future one. Not everyone is sincerely concerned with the wellbeing of your home and many of the people you share this information with may lose regard for your husband, or even your union long after you've resolved your issues and move on. You also do not want to be with your friends and repeatedly hear them bad mouth your husband, this might ruin your friendship with them and bring up unnecessary issues too. Having a therapist present will help put a check on outbursts and animosity that might arise from conversations and confessions. It is not everything your husband will open up to you about that you would be ready to hear, no matter how mentally prepared you think you are to take the hurt. Your husband is most likely sincerely sorry too, and will have to heal from the guilt and pain he is also going through. There might not be someone else he can open up to at this point, and you obviously will not be a good option too since some of his truth will only hurt you more. So a therapist is your best option. You have to understand that you and your partner are not exactly in a good state right now, and conversations will not likely go as planned. Accepting this and seeking help, is advised at this point.

iv) Draw out your Dos and Don'ts:

This is a phase where you're trying to rebuild your home again from ruins, and drawing out certain rules to help you both maintain the order till you're completely healed would contribute greatly. These rules are first to protect your union from third parties, but also to help you maintain your sanity while you heal. You can both decide to stay in separate rooms till you've ensured you're ready to share sincere intimacy again. Taking time off or staying away from other deeply emotional activities will keep your head clear while you seek help and spend time really talking. There are couples who make the mistake of trying to heal their union by using sex as a tool. This might feel good at the time, till you realize later on that you neglected certain vital steps, and trust, and complete healing have not yet been achieved. Trying to replace communication with sex and distractions at this point, will only drive you too fast and possibly awaken the hurt later in the future. So setting some rules and boundaries would be essential until you have completely recover. Your husband might be someone whose job description means he would always be around women. You might have been completely okay with this before now, but having found out his mistake, you might want certain adjustments to be made to make you comfortable again and if your husband is willing to achieve that with you, then it makes everything much better. Do not let your need for setting boundaries make you inconsiderate or unfair in the demands you make at this point. Understand that your husband has a career to fight for too, and make demands that are rational and not capable of ruining other aspects of his life. In setting boundaries with third parties, you have to understand that this will have to go both ways. Yes, it's true that it was your husband who made a mistake and not you, but the steps to making sure the mistake is not repeated again, is on the both of you. As he sets his boundaries with third parties, you do the same. As you state your demands and all the things that makes you uncomfortable, you give him room to do the same. Knowing that the both of you are taking equal steps to make your union work without putting blames in just one party, will create a feeling of partnership and not punishments. Your dos and don'ts should be firm, and be ready to cut connections with people who would pose as risks to your union in the future.

v)   Pray:

Many people ignore the importance of prayer during times when your strength has proven to fail you. A Christian home especially one laid on God's foundation will need the help of God to stand again after experiencing this shake. This does not mean that it is ever too late to turn to God if you've never involved Him in your marriage before. Praying together as you talk with your partner will produce great results and build a better bond for your union as you heal. There are also beautiful Christian books on how to build a happy home, how to cope with challenges in marriage, and how to recover from hurt when it arises in your union. Ultimately, there is the word of God. Making it a custom to pray and study together as a family, would build your bond more beautifully than you imagined. Many families tend to disregard how powerful a simple morning devotion in the family can be. That moment spent in singing together, praying, sharing dreams and experiences, is worth more than tons of gold. If you've gotten to a point where confusion and pain has overwhelmed you, this is a good time to revisit everything you can do better in your home, and to actually focus on doing them. Putting other things as a priority till you hit a rough spot is not the best option you have. Make your home your priority, put God first, and watch

Him rebuild every wall you believed could never be fixed again.

vi)   Spend time together:

There are activities you and your family can involve in to rebuild your bond and simply spend time together. Try taking trips together, indoor games, outdoor games, tours, concerts, chats, whatever it is you all enjoy doing together, this is the best time to revive those activities again. It is perfectly okay to involve your kids in this process as they may have sensed the tension between you and your partner already and giving them a reassurance that everything is returning back to normal, is completely healthy and should be a normal routine in your home. However, after these together time with your children, make it a priority to set aside time for just you and your husband. Go on dinner dates, shopping sprees, vacations. Spend time talking and sharing your deepest feelings. Remind yourselves of the dreams you both share together and how you plan to continue executing them. See movies, take strolls, involve in activities together. All of these intimate moments will help you and contribute greatly to the healing of your home. Don't rush anything, take things slowly and remember to make all of these natural activities that you and your spouse involve in together. A cheating doesn't always happen when it happens, it starts from the drifting away of both partners from themselves; the distance, the lack of communication, lack of emotional intimacy, and neglect or unavailability. So make it a culture to not go back to things that might give room to temptations and errors again.

vii)   Forgive:

All these efforts are targeted at one thing; giving your home a chance again. Harboring hatred and grudges will only hinder the process of finding healing for both yourself and your marriage. It is unrealistic to think that you will forget what has happened easily, no you won't. But it is very possible to forgive especially when your husband is genuinely sorry and wants to fix things. Let go of the hatred, the pain, the anger, the fury, the hurt, release them all from your heart. This is not just for the sake of your marriage, but for your own sake too. If you've decided to work on your home, you have to let go of your own pride and give all to make it work. A person who is truly sorry for their wrongs is worth giving another chance. This step comes in last because rushing to say you've forgiven too soon when you've not will turn out to cause more hurt in the future as the issue might arise again at a later time in your marriage, awakening all the pain and hurt that was buried in. So do not rush into this, but do not also push it away. You have to forgive to be able to move on, and yes it is possible to let go of all the hurt, and truly move on.

CHAPTER 6: TIPS FOR WOMEN WHO STAY WITH CHEATING HUSBANDS

TIPS FOR WOMEN WHO STAY WITH CHEATING HUSBANDS

i)   Get support:

At this point, you want to surround yourself with people you can trust and rely on. Don't try to go through this phase on your own, else you might break down. Being discreet with what you're going through does not apply to the cases of men who are unrepentant after being caught or who end up threatening their wives because she has found out the truth. If your husband poses a threat to your life or physically abused you while cheating on you, it is time to reach out for help. Inasmuch as there are agencies that extend support to domestically abused women, you can also reach out to a friend you can trust or a family member you can rely on, and get as much help as possible. Understand that your life is at risk here, and your home can still be saved when this issue of abuse has been addressed not before that. You have to fight for your life and for the purpose of being alive, especially if your union is blessed with children. You want to stay alive for your kids and not leave them in the hands of your husband and mistress if anything happens to you. If your husband refuses to change after being addressed and approached by people who are in positions to correct him, then it is wise of you to stay away from him till he comes to his senses. Your marriage is important, and so is your life.

ii)   Get a lawyer:

Even as you try to fix things, you should secure your stand and safety while you watch the progress of things. In cases where the husband is unrepentant, his next action might be to file for a divorce or to coerce the wife to grant him a divorce. As sad as this might be, it is not in all cases that the man is willing to fix the home or correct his mistakes and you would not want to be defenseless against your husband and his mistress if their intentions is to come after you. Get a lawyer, know your stand legally and what to expect if your husband decides to take the option of filing for divorce. This is even harder in a case where there are kids involved so the earlier you accept what is ahead of you, the more prepared you are to face whatever it is that comes. If you chose the option of reaching out to a foundation responsible for domestically abused women, they'll most likely take over the responsibility of getting you a lawyer or even press charges first against your husband for the abuse. Whichever way you choose to handle this, don't just sit on your hands and do nothing.

iii)   Do not hasten things:

If fortunately, your husband falls into the category of wanting to fix things, then it's wise for you to take things slowly at this point. This is a highly emotional point for you, and anger or hurt will likely push you to do things you might end up regretting. Do not try to make important decisions in a hurry for now, rethink things through before you act, weigh your options, and take time away to clear your mind if you feel the need for it. Time is a major factor in finding healing, even as you take the necessary steps to achieve this, don't expect anything to happen overnight. There are wives who make the mistake of letting their kids know of their husband's mistake when they are at the height of their emotions only to end up regretting their actions and the effect it ends up having on the children. Some cut ties with their husbands, only to realize in future that they could have forgiven him and moved on. There are those who also go after the other woman, only to end up complicating their own lives. This is not a time to act in a hurry, as you are very sensitive at this point and most of your decisions would be based on your emotions. Take things easy, be it fixing or leaving.

iv)   State your conditions:

Your husband would have to know that falling back to his extra marital affairs will come with consequences. Some men can be very unpredictable, so it is wise to make it plain to your husband that if the issue of cheating repeats itself in your marriage again, there would be consequences. This might be the first time you are having any issues of infidelity with your husband, and hopefully the last. It might also be that this has happened before, only to be repeating itself again now. Your husband needs to understand that if it happens again, he would not be let off the hook this easily again. Humans will naturally break laws if there are no punishments for violating them. This is not to say that your husband is someone who would intentionally want to hurt you, but the consciousness in his heart that he stands to lose something very great if he treads this path again, is necessary. Do not say things you know you're incapable of doing, but let there be a reasonable repercussion stated if he is ever found guilty of the act again. Going too extreme and making threats you know you will not be able to keep will make your word seem baseless when or if he defaults and you're unable to carry out your threat. State the rules and the consequences for breaking them, and move on. This can also be done legally with the help of a lawyer.

v)   Trust cautiously:

At this point, your husband is still under scrutiny and you have to let him know that it would take a while before you can trust him completely again.

Do not blindly believe the things he tells you for now, investigate them thoroughly, and slowly check his sincerity before you believe him again if he earns it.

There are men who would want to pressure you with their pleas to have things return to normal again. This is possible, but understand that it would take time before this happens again. In a case where the man is unrepentant and pretentious, he may only be trying to gain back your trust just so he can give you a bigger blow.

Be very careful and watchful of your husband's moves, activities, and learn to trust your instincts if you notice red flags again. Trust is earned not forced, so let your husband put in the efforts to gain back your trust again as it is very essential that trust is present in a marriage. Be sure to stay alert, as your safety is at stake in a case of continuous lies or deceit. Inasmuch as there are women who suddenly grow bitter at their husbands and do not want to trust or learn to love him again, there are also those who are desperate to have their homes return to normal. Women in this category might make the mistake of restoring complete trust in their husbands too soon, only to end up getting hurt again or even worse if his repentance was a lie.

vi)   Apply wisdom:

In a union blessed with children, dealing with cheating might be tougher considering the kids in all decision-making. Do not disclose your husband's unfaithfulness to your children especially if he is sincerely sorry and willing to change. You do not want to belittle him in front of his children or cause more awkwardness in your home as this might also affect them psychologically. Children tend to react more psychologically to issues in the home more than their parents are aware of.

No matter how hurt or angry you are, do not be selfish enough to ignore the wellbeing of your children just to take your revenge on your husband. Another area where wisdom is essential is in dealing with the extended families.

Your in-laws do not necessarily need to know that your husband made a mistake, neither does your own family. The grounds on which it is advised to involve third parties is in a case where your husband is unrepentant and also abusive. If you are in a marriage not fully approved by your own family and you have in-laws who love you truly, you might want to involve them first to prevent any extra drama that you are not in a position to absorb presently.

But if this is not the case and your family would be judicious with their actions, then reach out before your life is endangered further.

v) Consider yourself first:

It is true that your marriage is always worth fighting for, but once it gets to a point where it has become a threat to your wellbeing, do not make the mistake of keeping silent or taking no actions because you are bothered or embarrassed about what others would say.

There are men who mistreat their wives in private only to act as the ideal husband in public. Your marriage might have been praised and envied by all around you until this point, it is still not enough reason to decide to keep living the lie at your own detriment.

Let your wellbeing be your priority, not people's opinion. People are always eager to talk about recent happenings or criticize recent mistakes and even though it would hurt you to hear their hateful comments, decide to do what is ultimately best for you. People will talk for a while till they're tired or they find something new to rant about, but if you stay silent and lose your life in the process, you would have made the worst choice possible and would lose the chance to take charge of your life and gear it in the right direction.

Also remember that in choosing what's best for you, you are equally choosing what is best for your children knowing that they need you.

CHAPTER 7: HOW TO DEAL WITH THE PAINS OF BETRAYAL

HOW TO DEAL WITH THE PAINS OF BETRAYAL

Betrayal from friends usually would bore deep holes in our hearts and may even make us vow to never trust again. So imagine how much more painful it becomes when this hurt is coming from the very person we promised forever with. You would think that this betrayal would never go away and quite honestly, this is how it feels at first. All you can see at this point are traces of the lies, hurt, deceit and unfaithfulness. But with conscious efforts, you can move past the pain that comes from being betrayed, you can heal and gradually return your life to its normal course. Below are steps that will help you cope with the pain, and help you start your healing journey.

i)   Do not focus on the betrayal:

When we are hurt, we tend to spend a huge amount of our time mourning what was lost that we fail to see what can be saved. Focusing all your attention on the betrayal will not help you heal or move on, it would only hurt you deeper.

If you are sure what you're looking for is healing, then take your mind away from the betrayal and stop giving it so much space in your heart. As you gradually turn away your focus from how badly you were betrayed, you would begin to see possibilities ahead of you and your marriage.

Not focusing on the betrayal also helps you forgive your husband, and see how sorry he truly is. There is no way you can focus so much on the pain without obsessing about the other woman and trying to rationalize your husband's actions. You might only end up believing that it was your fault, and retiring to self-blame. This is not a time to make comparisons between yourself and your husband's mistress, it is a time to focus on just you and your wellbeing. Remember that this is not your fault, and there is nothing wrong with you.

ii) Let go:

It is one thing to take your mind away from the sins of your partner, it is another thing to completely let it go. Letting go here involves forgiving both him and his mistress, realizing that they're the ones who actually need pity for condescending so low, not you. If you had kept evidences of your husband's cheating, be it pictures, chats, items, throw them away or burn them. Keeping those things lying around would eventually interfere with your healing process as you may stumble into them occasionally.

As you dispose of the items physically, also let go of all the images you've stored in your mind mentally. If there's nothing to remind you of the acts of betrayal, it makes it easier for you to move on.

iii) Keep an open heart:

The mistake many people make after being betrayed is adopting the mindset that whoever they put their trust in, would always end up betraying them. This is not true, and may only end up making you cut people off your life even when they would have stayed true to you. The reason why you're striving for healing is because you need to be able to fully love and trust again.

So as you journey towards this healing, keep an open heart. Do not push people away from you, do not believe that everyone is the same. In this case, your husband if truly repentant and willing to earn your trust again, should be given another chance.

Do not decide to stay in your marriage with an adamant mindset of mistrust and grudges. You will have to learn to love your husband again, trust him, and allow him to love you again.

iv) Build Faith Again:

Faith is unwavering trust in a person, without doubts or questions. This might have been how strongly you had believed in your husband before he betrayed you. Taking gradual steps to rebuild it again is necessary.

This is not the only time your marriage is going to be faced with a challenge, and even though it wouldn't be the case of cheating again hopefully, you and your spouse will have to be strong together to overcome it.

Love becomes questionable if there is no trust to back it up but in a home where there is love and trust, strength and happiness is present. Building faith again in your husband and marriage, is all part of the steps of healing and reviving your marriage again.

No one says it's easy or should happen overnight, but make a conscious effort with your husband no matter how long it takes, to restore your marriage to where it used to be.

v) Move on:

It might take years of striving towards healing or months of joint efforts and communication before healing is actually achieved, and that's perfectly okay. After you find healing from the betrayal and begin to sense some normalcy return to your home, remember to move on like it never happened.

No one says the stigma of a mistake has to remain in your home forever. You and your spouse can decide that it never happened, and move on with complete bliss in your home. If it turns out that your husband was not willing to repent or cease from abusing you, it does not mean that your life should come to an end.

Move on, fight for other aspects of your life, focus on your children, build your career, involve in voluntary activities and reach out to the society. Your pain can become the reason why you stay down, or your motivation to rise.

The choice is always yours to make, and deciding to reach out to other women to show that a failed marriage does not mean a failed life, is another way to rise above your storms.

A large part of the society makes a woman feel that the only time she is accorded honor or respect is when she has a husband in her life, but this is not true. There are other profitable ways to live your life than staying in an abusive marriage.

You can move on from the hurt and betrayal; you can rewrite the script intended to bring you down; you can be all you ever aspired to be before you faced this challenge in your marriage.

Learning to move on after disappointments or setbacks always proves to be an issue to us as humans, but we can learn regardless how slowly. It is never easy to accept that a marriage you invested your whole life in is crashing before your face, but if your husband is unwilling to protect you and fix things, then it is not your fault and you may have to accept reality.

EXTRA NUGGET

No matter how anyone tries to undermine the pain you might be going through as a result of your husband's betrayal, the truth is it is a big deal.

Some women even go as far as wanting to take their lives when they found out that the person they trusted the most on earth, betrayed them. It is never going to be an easy journey to find out about your husband's infidelity and choose to recover from it. There are wives who found out too, and left without looking back.

Many people consider marriage infidelity a sin that can never be forgiven, but it is not true especially if the defaulter is sincerely sorry.

Many people who walk out of their marriages too fast end up regretting it and wishing to go back when it is already too late to reverse the actions taken. You can heal and you will heal with the right steps and determination to fix whatever went wrong in your home. Before you make any decision, remember that friends and family will not bear the responsibilities of your actions with you.

Remember that your children will be affected either positively or negatively by whatever you decide to do.

Remember that nobody's marriage is perfect and just because they do not share their own challenges with you, does not mean that things are all rosy on their sides.

Remember why you got married in the first place, and ask yourself if that reason is still worth anything to you.

Reconsider your partner, and why you chose him in the first place.

If all these thoughts give you a reason to take different actions than you would have taken just based on your emotions, then pay attention to them.

Every marriage will not heal in the same pattern, so be patient and let things take a natural course.

There might be other steps not mentioned here that you know might work for you and your partner, apply them.

Remember to trust your instincts and do what is ultimately best for your marriage and children, as these are your priority at this point.

CONCLUSION

In all, it won't be easy to handle the hurt of being betrayed or cheated on. It would take time, patience, love, and understanding.

It would take joint efforts, support and prayers. But in the end if your marriage is of value to you, then you would find all the sacrifices worth it.

Many cheating partners are sincerely sorry and would do anything to prove their genuine repentance. It is advised that you check the category your partner falls into after their mistake, and try to fix your home rather than end things if they're genuinely sorry.

Many homes have recovered and become even stronger and happier after an issue of infidelity. This does not mean that your husband has to cheat on you before you can work on making your marriage more beautiful, it only means that it doesn't matter what rough stage you face in your matrimony, healing is always possible.

All the steps listed here are aimed at helping you cope with the pain, and the process of finding healing and we hope sincerely that you find it.

Marriage is built on love, trust, commitment, patience, and determination. It would take two to make it work and finding a partner who is willing to fight for your union no matter the mistakes, is a blessing that should not be overlooked.

What cannot kill you they say makes you stronger. If your marriage can survive this, it can survive any other storm that might come its way. Many women also forget that it is only natural for humans to make mistakes and even though this is inexcusable, it is not always intentional and can be forgiven. We hope that all you have read here helps you, and plays a part in giving you the answers you need to overcome the hurt.

OTHER BOOKS BY THE SAME AUTHOR

1. 200 Ways to Seduce Your Husband: How to Boost Your Marriage Libido and Actually Enjoy Sex: A Couple's Intimacy Guide

2. 232 Questions for Couples: Romantic Relationship Conversation Starters for Connecting, Building Trust, and Emotional Intimacy

3. Communication in Marriage: How to Communicate Effectively With Your Spouse, Build Trust and Rekindle Love

4. Anger Management in Marriage: Ways to Control Your Emotions, Get Healed of Hurts & Respond to Offenses (Overcome Bad Temper)

To Help Your Spouse To Overcome & Recover Completely, While Improving Your Sexual Intimacy

10. How to Deal with A Difficult Spouse: Regain Control, Living with a Demanding, Manipulative, and Unappreciative Partner

11. How to Repair a Broken Marriage: Get Back On Your Feet, Bring Back the Lost Passion, And Cultivate a Better Relationship

12. How to Stay Married & Not Kill Your Spouse: Powerful Ways to Deal with Difficult Spouse, Cultivate Happiness in an Unhappy Marriage, & Boost Intimacy

13. How to Get a Divorce & Get Everything: Rules for Successful Separation,

Make the Right Decisions, & Build a Perfect Future

14. Couples Money Management Workbook: How to Handle Finances and Save Money for The Future

15. Surviving an Abusive Relationship: How to Deal with Verbal, Emotional & Physical Abuse in A Relationship

About the Author

Claire Robin is your ultimate relationship and life expert who specializes in counseling and relationship therapy. She has published several books on life and relationship which have created a visible impact on readers all over the world. Claire is currently on world tour, speaking at events and creating awareness about the essence of happy relationship and developing personal bliss.

Take Notes

_____

_____

_____

_____

_____

_____

_____

_____

_____

_____

_____

_____

_____

Take Notes

Take Notes

_____

_____

_____

_____

_____

_____

_____

_____

_____

_____

_____

_____

_____

Made in the USA
Las Vegas, NV
25 November 2024

12590842R00062